# TALES OF OBAMALAND

A collection of fables, myths, and
legends from a world not so far away

## ROBERT THOMAS

iUniverse, Inc.
New York   Bloomington

Tales of Obamaland
A collection of fables, myths, and legends from a world not so far away

iUniverse books may be ordered through booksellers or by contacting:

iUniverse
1663 Liberty Drive
Bloomington, IN 47403
www.iuniverse.com
1-800-Authors (1-800-288-4677)

ISBN: 978-1-4401-7466-7 (pbk)
ISBN: 978-1-4401-7465-0 (ebk)

Printed in the United States of America

iUniverse rev. date: 10/5/09

# Table of Contents

# Obamaland

The Land – carved by Almighty's hand
Its beauty laced with riches
Its coasts dressed in the whitest sand
Whose gnats supply grand itches.

The Land of Plenty, plenty 'nuff
For half the world to share
No care that they'd been draining stuff
And drains were stuffed with hair.

With people who'd played pretty rough
Not scared to take a hit
It helped their wills become right tough
It helped them learn to spit.

And spit they did when things got rough
Looked danger in the eye
Took every tough plight by the scruff
Refused to whine or cry

But lately seems they've drained their pool
A wave of uncool bosses
Spend too much time arranging duel
And drooling on their losses.

And fooling then became a sport
For all the horde to play
Be served up at the fake clay court
Sit back, enjoy the fray.

The Bells of Change began to ring
Scared birds out of their tree
Fear mongers somehow learned to sing
But sounded so off-key.

The amber waves of grain have browned
The grapes of wrath turned wine
New lion king has just been crowned
Now isn't that just fine.

He boasts to scare away the ghost
They toast to his success
While others fear they'll turn to toast
And who'll clean up the mess?

The king's quite savvy, ultra-slick
Perfected game of shell
Could sell a belle an ugly stick
Sell old fish that "don't smell".

Could make you think you're pretty smart
For spending time in gym.
Could make you think you let a fart
When that fart came from him.

There's tales spawned from this obtuse land
Have randomly got passed
Passed to tunes of a tuba band
Made Band Aides vacate fast.

And characters their moms could love
Quite sure…no one else will.
Just like a lovely soaring dove
Who's prepped to plop a pill.

# Gleeps v. Gronks

The Gleeps are king's supporters who
Would sleep with him, if wished
Emboldened by their new milieu
From years of pressure-squished.

Those Gleeps are quite a range of rogue
Elites with Jaguar cars
Some grace the cover page of Vogue
Some think as if from Mars.

They suffer from a guilt complex
As they'd grabbed fortune, fame
Left in their wake a quake of wrecks
From crisp deflects of blame.

So they fear they must make it up
To help them sleep at night.
On mission now to shake it up
And bake up this fake plight.

The Gleeps bow to John Maynard Keynes
They may have read Karl Marx.
Free marketers are such big pains
Unruly bunch of sharks.

But government can "solve it all"
Cuz bureaucrats are smart.
Have expertise to build a wall
On how to stall each start.

Gleeps wring their hands 'bout troubled world
'Bout sharing wealth and such
While keeping their stash safely squirreled
So sticky hands can't touch.

Gleeps think they're on some higher plain
Devoid of bothersome noise
And other details they distain
Like feigns and plain old ploys.

They're closeted professors, them
Who love to hear selves speak
Cuz each word's such a precious gem
That flows from their phlemmed beak.

They preach with evangelic flair
A scare of flailing arms.
And sporting Albert Einstein hair
And Homer Simpson charms.

The Gronks are conchs with heavy honks
Who just want to be Free
They work. They smirk. They're business wonks.
Gronks want to be let be.

So whisper words and let them be
This crew of wing-tip shoe
Don't hand to Gronks feng shui or ch'i
Don't rename old crust "new".

They're opposition…not so loyal
Now banished to back rows.
With blood temps fully set to boil
With each new proclaimed hose.

They parse King's tripped-up words, each phrase
Each blurb that they can pound
Each snippet put on loop replays
They'll quote the White House hound.

They'd rather not have oversight
Don't want Big Brother watching
Don't want that light to shine too bright
'Case there might be debauching.

But know must hammer slippery fiends
Who don't play by the rules
Who need to get their ashtrays cleaned
Of snuffed-out butts and drools.

The Gronks don't like the bail-out stuff
Hey, just let losers lose.
The losing toughens up their scruff
It's Nature's way to choose.

Unless that loss cuts close to home
Then glib rants all get hushed.
It's one thing to stir up some foam
Quite 'nother to get flushed.

They rail about Gleep spending sprees
Then go re-spend themselves
Abhor the thought of spending freeze
And cringe at spending delves.

The smart Gronks know just what it takes
Keep spending in control.
Stop sugar adds to frosty flakes
Stop pouring one more bowl.   (how droll!)

They love their guns, their Hum-V's, tanks
Love shanking 'em off tees
They fill their grilles with brats and franks
Go easy on the cheese.

They lobby for a strong defense
Say:  "One thing Feds do well"
Play games of Strategy Suspense
With goals:  Don't ask, don't tell.

The Gronks and Gleeps on fast track climbs
Just hate each other's guts
Accuse each other of high crimes
Accuse of breeding mutts.

Each has its own pet talking heads
Who bark loud at the moon.
Make sure these pit bulls stay on meds
So don't poop-out too soon.

They snarl, then gnarl at Postal-eers
Chase after old junk cars.
Poor common folk are bored to tears
From all the cat/dog wars.

And while they stir up groups of troops
The polarizing spreads
The spins are doing loop-de-loops
Like Exorcist's spun heads.

Exaggerate their differences
To help secure their turf
Impugn each others' references
With shots made out of Nerf.

As Gleeps and Gronks head toward their poles
And Angst-o-meter's maxxed
Both camps begin to search their souls
Souls that have been well-taxed.

The acrimony ratchets up
Each mole hill rises tall
Have started raising hatchets up
What's next?  You make the call.

Meanwhile…there in the back-row pews
Are Snooze-rods known as Smods.
The apathetics.  Krewe No Clue.
Pathetic habs of pods.

Tune out to all things off the farm
Blank face the issues/trends.
Forget to set their own alarm
No enemies…no friends.

Dislike the Gleeps for what they do
And Gronks for what they don't.
Smods can't tell what is really true
Nor spot lies finely honed.

At end of day, they couldn't care less
And surely couldn't care more.
Let others muddle in the mess
While Smods perfect their snore.


But this day, o'er in Syracuse
The Smodsters stage a "March"
More like a "Crawl on Syracuse"
Decked out in "Hold the starch"

Some had just come off their commode
And set aside their files
'Bout 30-40 people showed
Some driving 3-4 miles.

They claimed that they were Nothingists
Philosophy d' Noir
A brand new wave of sluffing-ists
Lethargy pledge, they've swore.

Their motto is:  Go Figger it out
And please don't bother us.
Be on the porch with jiggers of stout
In fogs devoid of fuss.

With mascot of a sleeping dog
Who would not wake if kicked.
As simple as to fall off log
Too tired to be too ticked.

Reporter from the Local News
Showed up...slow day in Crimes
Could be big news in Syracuse
Had to be woke 3 times.

They want Inaction Bill of Rights
That guards against new laws
Want sidewalks promptly rolled at nights
And why?  Well…just because.

Had thought 'bout a 3$^{rd}$ party run
E'en though it might seem crazy
But turned out when all said and done
The guys were just too lazy.

The rally broke on Headline News
As some news quirk…a lark
But pundits worried Syracuse
Might light up some new spark.

The more they tried dissecting it
The 'fraider they became.
They tried so hard deflecting it
That it gave Smods new fame.

Became obsessed with this fresh drive
This Undrive Drive grass root
Symposium of Anti-strive
Hive of:  Don't Give a Hoot.

E'ery now and then, they'd find a Smod
Who was not 'fraid to speak
He'd rail 'bout how the Smods' been trod
Just cuz their zeal's so weak.

Said:  We want fiscal nothingness
Start over every year
No earmarks, skidmarks…all that mess
Tax rules that aren't unclear

Stop fighting stupid Mideast wars
Let those nuts kill themselves
Stop opening…start closing doors
Let's focus on ourselves

Want social program nothingness
Stop legislating morals.
Stay out of people's bus-i-ness
Go off and sniff some florals.

This kind of talk was much too much
For all the Gronks and Gleeps
Freaked out that nerves might feel this touch
Among the nation's peeps.

Both camps, quite independently
Concluded:  This must stop!
We can't have all this fancy free
Our loyal base might drop…

(to be continued)

# The Freshman and the Buffalo

The Freshman's Crown Vic belching smoke
Coughs into Merford's lot.
Thought many times ole Vic might croak
From some low-octane clot.

The old sled, now on life support
Still somehow got him here
To this high-fangled court, of sort,
That's been stuck in low gear.

Chock full of vinegar and wiz
His gizzard tightly wrenched
And nose hairs that will start to frizz
When his butt gets unbenched.

He promised that he'd change this dump
On each stump on his path.
A new class to de-frump each chump
And dish out clumps of wrath.

The Freshman shuffles 'long the mall
Sees something chewing grass.
A buffalo with southern drawl
Seems talking out his ass.

Come here, Son.  Welcome to our Club.
We're so glad y'all have come.
I'll watch your bum, so you won't flub
Nor fumble, nor look dumb.

Was that a voice?  Or was it fart?
Sometimes it's hard to tell
So hard to tell the two apart
When both of them so smell.

I've seen you Freshmen come and go
So many, many years.
So many Freshmen stub their toe
And drag butts home in tears.

But I sense <u>you're</u> cut from good cloth
So I'll give you my hoof
So your cloth won't infest with moth
Make you look like a goof.

Well…thanks…I guess.  But I must say
I'm here with goals to shake.
And bake those old ways stuck in clay
I've got some coals to rake.

That's great!  Man, that's what these guys need.
Such spirit, such gung ho!
Go tackle all that graft and greed.
Go pick that fruit hung low.

But if you need some good advice
I'll be here grazing grass.
Won't have to ask me twice or thrice.
Won't slice you up with sass.

For starts…the normal dress code rule
At sessions:  3-piece suits.
Those tailored suits, they look so cool
'Cept when Texans wear boots.

The two part ways, drift in the haze
Frosh thought he'd made a friend
To help him deal with such malaise
Someone he could depend.

Next day, the Freshman went to work
Spiffed in gray pin-stripe suit.
Exuding air of anti-jerk
My, my…he looks astute.

When he arrived, to his surprise
His comrades were in shorts
And T-shirts sporting pink tie-dyes
Blue ball caps of all sorts.

He gazed around the room then notes
Not one dude dressed in suit.
No vests, no ties…he eyes no coats
The Freshman looked the fruit.

> That freaking buffalo, that troll!
> That a-hole got me conned.
> I just paid one enormous toll
> Just cuz of what I donned!

That evening, steaming, tracked him down
Found in brown patch of rye
With arm flails like some Barnum clown
And thermostat on "fry".

> He cussed the Buff: "Your 'help' went bust…
> Disgusted's how I feel.
> The dress code's <u>not</u> what you discussed
> You made me feel a heel.

You suited up in casual week?
Must've been one cheeky demo.
Why would you doll up like a geek?
Did you not see the memo?

What "memo" are you squawking 'bout?
Have you been eating roots?
You 'splained the dress code – left no doubt
You told me 3-piece suits.

I told you suits were <u>normal</u> wear
And ladies wear dress skirts.
But Cazh week they let down their hair
And don the surf shop shirts.

You've got to read the posted notes
Or be Out of the Loop.
Be careful….they'll be taking votes
While you step out to poop.

Okay, perhaps I got it wrong
But still feel semi-hosed.
I swear, I felt like Cheech and Chong
Whose last act just got closed.

What wisdom next will you impart?
And what can I believe?
For filthy beast, you're pretty smart.
What's up your hairy sleeve?

I'd say Stand Tall what you believe
On your two little feet.
The only way that you'll achieve
Respect:  Must stand the heat.

Go <u>argue</u> with the leadership.
Show you can't get pushed under.
Show them you're not some Freshman drip
Who goes from blund to blunder.

Next week, the Leaders sailing through
A fast-tracked new hot bill…
Mass transit for Detroit?  What?  Who?
More pork fest on the Hill?

Twelve billion dollar "Aeroflot"?
Some transport with transfat?
With arteries so clogged with clot
One Freshman yelling:  Stat!

      Detroit's the <u>Motor City</u>, guys
      Those Mo-Joes love their cars.
      Not packed in train cars swatting flies
      And smoking bad cigars.

      I <u>protest</u> spending that much dough
      On such un-needs, un-wants.
      Let's give this Bill the ole heave ho
      I'll wait for your response.

            Who's that loud Leader of the Mob??
            Oh, you….it's Mister Suit.
            The arrogant, suit-doffing snob
            And bonus… also rude.

            I guess they don't teach manners, Son
            In your pathetic town.
            Your brash-burger is overdone.
            Your eyeballs just turned brown.

A foe of the Environment!!
Don't care if they pollute?
A stewardship retirement.
You just don't give a hoot!

I reckon you're just anti-green…
No green from head-to-toe.
That doesn't mean you should be mean
To those poor folks in Mo.

The Freshman shlumped toward home that eve
Well beaten down, well squished.
He wore his heartbreak on his sleeve
Sure's not the weave he'd wished.

Then, in the mist…the Buffalo
Stooped down to pinch a deuce.
Unflushed, unrushed. Just take it slow
Unfettered, feeling loose.

Hey, Cow Pie…Yeah, you got me screwed.
Advice that smells like…THAT!
(Cough, cough) You need to change your food
Retain the trash you spat.

You told me: "Argue with the Whip.
Get in the Whipster's face.
They love debates. They hate a drip.
They'll rip the basket case."

So Argue's what this Freshman did
'Bout that dumb transit bill.
Your strategy then hit the skid
When they brought out the drill.

When you went in and told the Whip
That you were gonna protest…
Gave him heads-up so he'd not flip…
See anything you noticed?

Example:  did you see him cringe
Or see his eye balls spin?
Did his stare make you ear hairs singe
Or peel off grafts of skin?

Well…errr…I did not pre-review
My thoughts or tarts with him.
Just took the Floor.  And foo, man, flew.
I did it on a whim.

No, no, no, Man.  You can't do that!
It's all about respect.
You gotta learn to tip your hat
Before you get erect.

Thought you'd <u>know</u> "common courtesy"
To warn before you scorn.
Before you burp a blurt, ya' see
Before you blast your horn.

I guess, I s'pose, I could forewarn
Preclude a Floor blaze-up
This whole thing's got my senses torn.
I'm not sure which way's up.

Okay….here's way to save your hide.
Show them you're on the team
You need some way to turn this tide
And I've got just the scheme.

This Friday, they will ask the Frosh
To get up on the Table
And dance the Macarena…gosh
I hope these tabes arc stable.

It's just Tradition…breaks the ice
Just all in good clean fun
I hear they treat the Rookies nice
The fry's not too well done.

Get on that table – take the Lead
Get up and, man, get down.
Show dance moves like some crazy steed
And grab that Dance Man crown.

You must be kidding….table dance?
Can I keep on my clothes?
Sounds like something they'd do in France
To show off painted toes.

I'm telling you…this _is_ your chance
Come down from your high horse.
You will not have to drop your pants
Unless you wish, of course.

Hey, listen... thanks for all your help
It's late, I must be off.
If I need help, I'll yell or yelp,
Or sneeze, fart, belch, or cough.

They parted ways, the Freshman crazed.
"Been set up from Day One.
This new one's got my saddle blazed
For me to be made fun."


On Friday, sure 'nuff, Leader speaks
Calls all the Frosh to dance.
Get on those tables, shake those cheeks
The sound of Latin bands.

He looks around, but no one stands
Eyes gazing off afar.
The Freshmen chairs are glued to cans.
It's just too danged bizarre.

The stillness of unmoving feet
The tension almost stuns.
Then one young gun gets off his seat
And starts to shake his buns.

Another joins, and then one more
The crowd starts going wild.
The rhythms drowned out by the roar
Just gets our Friend more riled.

It's still a set-up...least I think...?
I get up... they'll all laugh.
Just look... does not this dancing stink?
Is this how you spell 'gaffe'?

I must admit:  they've played this out
Continuing trite joke.
I don't see what they're chortling 'bout
Must had too much to smoke.

When ends, the Whip comes up to him
Asks:  "You too good for this?
Too good to get out on this limb?
Too full of your own piss?

To arrogant to drop your hair?
Too anal to have fun?
Too square to jump up on your chair
And get yourself undone?"

Dejected, Fresh-guy walked the Mall
His face of record length.
An ego shrunk to ultra-small.
Limp gut devoid of strength.

And sure enough ole Buffalo
Was dining on his path.
A smirk, a wink, a shuffalo
But still in need of bath.

He thought – Oh great, that's all I need
One more rub in my face.
One more snub, more piranha feed.
One more chunk to debase.

Instead the Buffalo was meek
A sense of sympathy
A knowledge of what's up Shmitt's Creek
To aid his wimpathy.

It's tough for you guys…so brand new
Not knowing all these ropes.
The sorting of the glue from goo
And dealing with these dopes.

But trust me, Son.  You'll be all right.
This Freshman dance will stop.
There'll be a time to fight your fight
And you'll come out on top.

Buff went on, talked 'bout other guys
Who first tripped, then made big.
Kept trusted friends who sorted lies
Would warn:  beware of pig.

The Freshman felt a burden lift
A bounce back in his step.
New path so as to not get stiffed
A dash of newfound pep.

He thanked the Buffalo and danced
The Latin Hustle home
Return of almost-lost romance
Reprieve from trip to Nome.

Two blocks behind, the Whip just watched
The disco-dancing dude.
    "Looks like the Frosh has just got scotched…
    A certain change of mood."

    Hello, Sir.  It's a pleasant night."
    The Buffalo replies.
    "The chance of rain is not in sight.
    So good to see clear skies."

You're right, Buff.  We've had enough rain.
Want to get on my boat.
Been so long…'bout to go insane
I hope it will still float.

So how are things up on the Hill?
How goes the daily drill?
Got votes on that new spending bill?
What is it…half a trill?

It's close.  The other side objects
They say it costs too much.
They spend their time dissecting specks
Like earmarks, pork, and such.

So how's things with our new boy there?
Didn't want to over-taunt him…
I'd say we truly tamed that bear.
We got him where we want him.

# The Mayor's Parking Spot

"No Way," the chunky cherub glubbed.
"I swear I did not do it."
A fitful try to get hands scrubbed
While thinking:   Man, I blew it.

And thinks:  How'd I get in this jam?
I'm such a well-liked guy.
I don't deserve this plate of spam
Stuffed up my open fly.

The Newsgirl has her pencil cocked
A notepad perched to jot.
With questions certain to get blocked
By this old cagy snot.

They said he sold his parking space
Down front of City Hall
In some space race that <u>so</u> lacked grace
Five hundred bucks… that's all ???

Who'd sell a stupid parking spot?
Makes not one lick of sense.
Who'd buy that spot in that odd lot?
Is any clod that dense?

So Mister Mayor, tell me Sir…
Five hundred dollar slot?
A smoke screen!!!  This did not occur.
I cooked-up no such plot.

But Sir, you're there… on video tape
Five crisp bills <u>did</u> change hands.
  Was 5 bucks for a touch of grape
  Tastes like it came from France.

Eight witnesses have just come forth
Claimed you proposed this sale.
  They're liars…liars…from up North
  That's why they look so pale.

They've all filed affidavits, Sir
They filed today in Court.
  They're perjurers who wear faux fur
  They grrrr because they're short.

I saw the Painters at your curb
Were white-washing your name.
  A punk defaced it with some blurb
  Graffiti… such a shame.

You left a clear-cut email trail
Soliciting space bids.
  Those hacker creeps… they never fail
  Should go arrest those kids.

  That City Clerk…he wants my job
  Been eyeing it for weeks.
  Conniving little creaky slob
  Comes from a clan of freaks.

The City Clerk's an honest man
He never ran for mayor
So down-to-earth.  The guy eats bran.
Your job is not his care.

It's one gol-dern conspiracy
These jerk-bags are so jealous.
This set-up's such a fallacy
Can't trust one thing they tell us.

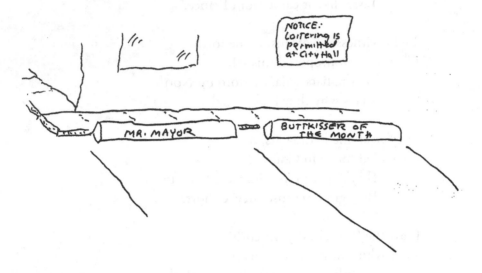

You sold your freaking parking spot!
Conspiracy?  Say what??
You put 5 C-notes in your pot…
Put your pot in this rut.

I did not sell it.  Read my lips.
You News Folks are so mean.
Fake news to justify your trips…
Fake trips to grab more green.

So, Sir, will you be parking there?
Your car be there at morn?
My sick car's in the auto care
My poor front seat's been torn.

So, space will be unoccupied?
I hate to split more hairs…
        You might see someone else's ride…
        I s'pose… who knows… who cares?

Might see a car from some old guy
Who's 'bout 500 short?
        Please don't rely on lying guy
        Whom I would not consort.

I'm sorry, Sir, but let me say
You must think we're all putz.
This evidence:  no shades of gray
Case opens, Sir.  Case shuts.

        Well even if I did what's told
        (Of course, which I deny)
        There's no law says it can't be sold
        Go check the books, then sigh.

        You're giving me 6 tons of flack
        You quack 'bout laws not written
        You're leading this pit bull attack
        Press on till I'm well bitten.

        Why must you slicksters pick on me?
        Hey, I'm a Family man.
        A wife, 2 kids, and cats times 3
        With names Freak, Frock, and Fran.

        I pay my taxes, go to church
        Shop local yokel stores.
        Now here comes effort to besmirch
        My good name with cold sores.

Guess this is what it's all become:
Pan fry the poor Good Guy.
Just pass around that Glass of Glum
Goes good with Mumble Pie.

They talk Impeachment on the street
Your comment, Sir, on that?
      Peach-mint?  Sounds like some chocolate treat.
      I'm dieting… low fat.

      So no peach-mint for me, no thanks.
      Maybe a Caesar salad.
      And one small side of beans and franks
      That's dashed with herbs and shallot.

I left my cater truck at home
I've packed no steak or tater.
I'm so bored that I wrote a poem
May tell it to you later.

Forgot just why I came down here
You've caused my brain to snap.
It's getting tough to persevere
I think this thing's a wrap.

He heads on back to City Hall
He's brushed off this lame grill.
No way he's gonna take a fall
Claims innocence, yet still.

He closes the oak office door
Dismisses thought of prayer.
He wonders how much more's in store
Plops down in beat-up chair.

He plays with stress ball on his desk
That's been well-squeezed before.
Moves coffee cup that's got grotesque
Then opens top desk drawer.

Drawer's full of papers wheeled-and-dealed
On top's the one he'll seek
A Lease Agreement signed and sealed
Pays him 10 bucks a week.

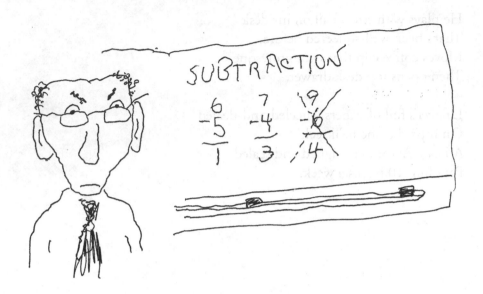

# Subtraction Class

Attention please.  Attention class.
Sure are one raucous bunch.
I've never seen a class so crass
Before they've eaten lunch.

They say you people are the cream.
A congress… hundreds strong
Dysfunctioned team of high esteem
That seems to do things wrong.

But thanks to Experts, they've found out
Why you folks should be thwacked.
You're missing one key skill, no doubt
Don't know how to <u>Subtract.</u>

Subtract… it's part of Basic Math
The opposite of Add.
I'll tutor you along this path
Might even see a grad.

Professor… I am <u>so</u> confused…
This whole "subtraction" ruse
That Math class… guess I might have snoozed
From night of too much booze.

So how exactly do you do
This thing you call subtract?
Is this some trick, some slight of shoe?
Some half-baked magic act?

No, no… let's say you have 4 trees
And then chain-saw one down.
So let's subtract – you're left with three.
Have all you got that down?

I don't see why you'd cut that tree
That's home for squirrels and birds.
Don't you care 'bout Ecology
Or all those Eco-nerds?

Took 50 years to grow that tree
Yeah, sure, there's billion more
And sure they grow back naturally
Just something I abhor.

Oh, please don't think of cutting trees
Been 'nuff deforestation
There needs to be a trees-cut freeze
And be more tree plantation.

Okay – let me try something diff.
Start with 6 Mary-Janes.
The candy that's a tad bit stiff…
Eat one, then what remains?

       I'm on the diet from South Beach
       I can't eat even one.
       I try to keep sweets out of reach
       Obesity's no fun.

    I never liked those Mary Janes
    One time I broke a tooth.
    My whole head was engulfed in pain
    Yelled out things rude, uncouth.

       They sell them at this antique store
       Right next to bins of junk.
       Been sittin' there since '54
       That bin just kinda stunk.

Forget the trees and Mary Jane
Please, gang, let's stay on point.
Your learning skills are quite inane
You stinkin' up the joint.

Subtraction… come, let's try again.
Let's say you've got 3 boys
And one skips off from where he's been…
Who's left to make the noise?

       Was he abducted?  Kidnapped?  Grabbed?
       This sounds so sinister.
       Did he get knifed, or poked, or jabbed?
       May call his minister.

Where were his parents in this skip?
Guess nowhere to be found.
Were prob'ly on some whirlwind trip
While their son's gagged and bound.

Where are the Cops in all this mess?
Need All Points bulletins.
The Doughnut shop would be my guess
Rebulking skeletons.

Forget about the missing boy!
It's just 3 minus 1.
So simple… not some crazy ploy
Subtraction… just have Fun.

Say… you sold Fred a pint of swill
You asked for seven skins.
And Fred gave you a 10-buck bill
What change comes from twin fins?

I'd prob'ly let Fred keep the change
Would be just like a tip.
Help rid him of his case of mange
And his disgusting drip.

I don't drink liquor, not a drop
Would <u>not</u> be selling booze.
Won't fill my throat with one mere hop
Refuse to "pay my dues".

One time I bought rum from a friend.
Man, that was a mistake.
Spent all night doin' the porcelain bend.
Quakes caused my kids to wake.

But, Class… let's just say if you did…
Can you just do the Math?
Sub any product sold instead
Perhaps one with less wrath.

> I'd like to sell Fred some old bike
> Like one he sold to me.
> Was made back in the term of Ike
> That wreck threw out my knee.

> Should not sell good friends anything.
> It's one big Danger sign.
> Sell folks whose necks you'd like to wring
> The few, the loud, the swine.

Subtraction concept seems to breed
Hostility in you.
It's like some lude, crude frenzy feed
Can feel the anger brew.

> Have you tried all those brews at Chuck's?
> Should try that new pale ale.
> That place is such a nest of shmucks
> Whose burps make their air stale.

> Remember when Chuck's was the place…
> Martinis for a buck?
> Could not find one square foot of space…
> Was barely space for Chuck.

It's clear this group need be regrouped
You're tougher than imagined.
I tell you, gang… I'm getting pooped
From all your flies off-tangent.

Now here's nine apples… can you hear?
I take one off the crate…
How many are left sitting here?
How many left… how…
                              "Eight".

Who said Eight?  Who expelled that word?
My, my, my… who said Eight?
Who's rose above this numbing state?
Who's parted from Nerd-herd?

                    You ate the apple.  That is why
                    The apple isn't there.
                    Don't blame you…thoughts of apple pie
                    Since I plopped in this chair.

What?  Ate the apple?  What'd you say?
Did you say ate or eight?
Please say, before my hair turns gray,
That what you said was Eight.

                    I ate 2 apples yesterday
                    Or… hmmm… the day before.
                    They're good sliced, stewed, sauced, anyway
                    Could almost wolf the core.

Class…  Let me try another way
The concept of Subtract.
It's when you take something away
Or when something gets whacked.

                    That sounds so Anti-merican
                    And someone will get hurt.
                    Man, this is not Uzbekistan
                    Who're happy in their dirt.

My life's been one big takeaway…
You can't have this, not that.
You want a bonus?  Start to pray.
Go befriend some fat cat.

I think my grampaw spoke of this
"Subtraction" thing, years past
He gassed about the funds they'd piss
Would fuss:  this muss can't last.

No clue what that old geezer meant
Suspect was getting senile.
His head was formed of hard cement
From years and years of denial.

I used to know how to subtract…
At least, I think I did.
I guess that mem'ry bank has blacked
Beneath this well-coffed lid.

"Reduce"…  Was that a word they used?
Weird phrase like:  "Cut in Half"…?
Sounds funny now.  Keeps me amused.
It almost makes me laugh.

Subtract:  A word like "buggy whip"
Two words whose time has passed.
Like some old ad for Nasal Drip
Relief that's fast, Fast, FAST!

Has zip to do with nasal drip!
C'mon guys.  Try real hard.
Let up.  Reset your brain pow'r trip.
Dig through that skull of lard.

I see the blank looks on each face
I know your handicaps.
Years past, you knew how to erase.
Unused, caused it to lapse.

I'm 'fraid this ends our class.  Time flies.
Believe we've made a start.
I see <u>relief</u> in all your eyes...
Did someone let a ........?

# The Antarctica Situation

We interrupt your programming
Must bring this Flash of News
A Penguin flap is emerging:
"Antarctica lit fuse".

A global crisis could ensue
Our troops are on Alerts
So suddenly this crisis grew
Among these waddling squirts.

Tried getting newsfolk on the scene
But it's so freaking cold.
Plus those darn birds have gotten mean
Our weatherman got rolled.

The Emperors have taken charge
Subdued the ornery Kings.
Crushed Little Blues, who aren't so large
Pulled out their little wings.

"That's racial cleansing in my book"
Said Secretary Bird.
"The CIA must take a look…
And cook this hawk-like herd."

Reportedly are hording fish
Make others eat iced-bugs.
Those squished bugs make one nasty dish
I hope they cull out slugs.

They've set up work camps for Chin Straps
Build igloo homes of snow.
In case the melt of Polar Caps
Cause beach front homes to flow.

Must work all day and half the night
Flap snowballs with their wings.
It seems a mapless, hapless plight
To make these spiteful things.

And then, the thing that we fear most
The wep of mass destruction.
Chem warfare on the Weddell Coast
Preventing airpath suction.

A million penguins, upturned ass
Across Antarctic nation
Delivering their toxic gas
It's true mass flatulation.

Enough to kill the Ozone zone
Been known to change the weather.
So strong, could dissolve femur bone
Turn feather into leather.

Creates some kind of imbalance
Of what… I'm not quite sure
A risk … no, Fear… of global trance
With, as yet, no known cure.

Been found importing high-tech fuel
Lug boxes off strange ships
Hang by the heavy water pool
And stuff down nacho chips.

They're learning how to march like Ducks
A clearly complex notion
Puts musco-skeletons in flux
True flummoxed in this notion.

Some ne'er-do-wells just Warble march
Which makes them look like shmucks
With legs that look of too much starch
Large keisters packed with tucks.

Their leader, Paydolf Penguin, shouts:
Arf narf farf garf glarf snarf !!
Have no clue what he's arfing 'bout
Have not been trained in Arf.

Seems charismatic in his arfs
His subjects well engaged.
Big trouble if one coughs or barfs
Two seconds…be encaged.

Wiped out the 'guins with sawed-off beaks
Genetic beak-depress.
They neutered 'guins whose bottom leaks
Guess they make too much mess.

They took the 'guins that smelled too bad
And ones that smelled too good
Marched over to the launching pad
Formed missiles of shark food.

They turned some into penguin bisque
Whose feathers are dark brown.
"Off-color puts us all at risk
As predators swoop down."

"We must protect our fragile gene"
Black-feathered throng decries.
"Not like we're trying to be mean.
On contrary… we're wise."

It seems they think they're special birds
Oh my, how times have changed.
Not long ago were uber-nerds…
Have sure become deranged.

Turned tables on the Seal herds
Just shooed them off their lands.
Embarrassed to be beat by birds
They all struck off for France.

"Those dumb seals were such lazy brutes.
They scarfed up all our fish.
We've hated all their flops and scoots
Incessant sound of squish."

Let's hear from Don in Washington
The White House... what say they?
World waits to see how this gets spun
From Rumplestiltskin's hay.

The NSC has met since three
When all got back from lunch.
Deliberating strategy
In dealing with that bunch.

One group says:  Let's negotiate.
Try get Penguins to reason.
Another says:  Annihilate...
This ain't the reason season.

The Air Force chief gave his reply:
"Attack now.  No more messin'.
Those nasty birds can't even fly.
Let's teach those guys a lesson.

"Let's blast them all to kingdom come
To tunes of:  Take you higher.
Let's drop a megaton stink bomb
That spells:  fight fire with fire."

The Doves said:  "No attack, let's talk.
Let's find out what they want.
Before we turn them into chalk
With all this hyper-vaunt.

Those 'Guins may have legit concerns
That we must understand.
That's causing all these red-ass burns
They might just need a hand.

Must think of Seals now on the run.
Where will these blubbos go?
Who will accept these tons of fun…
Who now are tons of woe?

These infights, squabbles, stabs of back…
The President's perplexed
And pundits loading trucks of flack
Could get a sane man vexed.

Right then, a lonely voice comes fore.
    "What if we just did zip?
    Did nothing, nada, love, nix, nor.
    Let penguin lids just flip.

    We have no dog in this cock fight.
    Led by birds who shout: Heil.
    Besides, this year our Budget's tight
    Let's spend on what's worthwhile.

    Imagine, folks, the cleanup mess
    The miles of penguin guano.
    The cost of moon suits, troop duress,
    The chides from guys like Bono.

    Let Nature's forces run its course
    Without our "helping hand".
    Our hand can only make it worse
    While stumbling to remand.

        I guess we could just let things lie…?
        Nawww… not the 'Merican way!!
        Let's get back to what Wedge to try
        Must act with no delay.

The Natural World… they count on us
To intervene when needed.
Inoculate each glob of pus.
Expunge each weed that's seeded.

Just think of how the world be changed
If <u>we</u> were here years back.
Those life forms that became estranged
Might not have gotten whacked.

Now… let's get back to strategy…
Those stink bombs…are they armed?
The gas masks…….

# The Associated Crime Lovers Union Resort & Spa

They'd rehabbed relics in the past
And made them stunning marvels.
But this vast mass is unsurpassed
Besides it smells so arful.

To redesign the Classic "Joint"
An architect's true honor.
Which sits right off of Frisco's point
This test won't be a yawner.

Their vision:  a famed theme resort
For crooks across the land
For killers, burglars, crimes of tort
All sorts of the ex-canned.

Bought up the Isle of Alcatraz
Raw beauty so unmatched
Paid half a song for pile that has
Potential to be hatched.

And hatched a criminal work of art
Designed to fit all needs
Gave old junk piles a brand new start
And custom-cropped the weeds.

It took each ounce of right-brain gel
To transform the ole Rock.
Took Clorox tanks to kill the smell
And drills to bust the hock.

The CLU Resort and Spa
A spacious new oasis.
Can carve away the crime day blah
Or carve your buddies' faces.

The owners, as most people know
Defend the rights of crooks.
To help the country's drugs to flow
And steady stream of hooks.

The architects designed the Spa
With rich amenities
Snuck in some little bits of awe
Before embezzling freeze.

Such as the Traz new training wing
Has 40 training rooms
With accents grabbed from Ossining
Adds Zing Zing to old tombs.

Crook training was an urgent need
So Traz beefed up its staff.
Recruited the most mutant seed
Whose brains have shrunk by half.

The trend in night-time robbery
Has fallen off this year
Techniques done too improperly
Have squelched that spread of fear.

Traz will rebuild that base of skill
Sharp skills:  How Best to Rob.
That prowling, sneaky cat-like drill
It's more than just a job.

And yes, will get true experts back
The crooks who wrote the book.
Who, honestly, just have the knack
To pull jobs like a Cook.

For thieves who've spent some time in can
Just got back on the street
Retrain you as a lookout man
To help peep out the Heat.

Help crooks rob old Convenience stores
Before forgetting how
Can train them how to double scores
In favorite crook cash cow.

Down hall… Pickpocket Fitness Club
Will sharpen wallet nabs.
The train gang helps crooks snatch and rub
And quicken pocket stabs.

Revives lost lack-of-nimble touch
Shares new tips on watch peelings
This Fitness plan won't cost too much
Dutch funds it with his stealings.

Try Bad Aromatherapy
Of rotten egg, so skunky
The nasty scents will set you free
To be a free-bird flunky.

The Stair Machines will build-up legs
For all those Upstairs heists
Can even help feists who've got pegs
Five-finger discount priced.

Know most top crooks are lazy boned
Who've done no stitch of work
Here:  Beer guts are considered "toned"
Well-sculpt by years of shirk.

Designers built a swimming pool
That once was Cell Block 3
That green spot is Capone's old drool
The yellow spot's his pee.

Can platform dive from Birdman's perch
Can still see withered feathers
And if guests grope, scope, probe, and search
Might find Bird's hidden leathers.

All join the gang and play Dirt Ball
Like volleyball… in Mud.
There's so much filth, all have to crawl
To find the ball in crud.

Can sunbathe in Traz musty fog
Let mud dry till it's crusted
To show to all your inner hog…
Your momma'd be disgusted.

Most guests will like to hit the Beach
Pack picnic lunch to eat
May see escaped cons, skin-tone: bleached
Come wash up at their feet.

Built fine cool bars 'round every bend
Cuz most the guests are drunks
Want frauds to know they've got a friend
Their motto:  We be Punks.

Those mugs from Rehab…we'll unhab
With pitchers of free beer.
We're sick of all that psycho-bab
And sick of lo-cal beer.

Traz restaurants serve "Old Prison" fare
Like gravy slopped in bread.
And beans well-laced with curly hair
That Rock ex-guests have shed.

At night will read Miranda Rights
Our Bible 'fore lights out.
Dream 'bout cops dancing in their tights
As crooks twist them about.

Yes, Traz resort has filled a niche
That never has been filled.
A place where every bastard, bitch
Can come, and not get killed.

Brought to you by The CLU
Where crime's a state of mind.
Who're always there to stand by you
While watching your behind.

# The Bridge to Nowhere: Dedication Ceremony

McGrotch again stares at his watch
Two minutes since last check
Career can't withstand one more botch
He strokes, then chokes his neck.

Steps up upon the makeshift stage
And peers down Wagecut Road.
Represses his strong urge to rage
Teens wage that he'll implode

The Bridge to Nowhere's stainless steel
Is glistening in the sun
With no one asking:  What's the Deal?
Why dampen all this fun?

The free beer's flowed since four o'clock
Most patrons are half-stiff.
Got discount kegs of Sniffbird Bock.
Tastes bad, but what's the diff?

But hors d'oevres did not make it yet
No cocktail weenie nubs
Won't add much to the National Debt
Got volume discount grubs.

At last, here comes a cloud of dust
That slaloms Wagecut potholes
Dust may get his comb-over mussed
May plug up both his snot-holes.

Hizzoner, dressed like Bronco Buck
A clearly dressed-down look
Shows off his Lincoln pickup truck
That's chauffeured by a crook.

What kind of message does <u>this</u> send?
It really doesn't matter.
Folks care more 'bout who will bartend
Rebuff foiled fluffs of flatter.

A paid-off ad hoc marching band
Plays some old march from Sousa
While citizens all dart and stand
To start this hullabalooza.

They'd rather be down at Wal-Mart
Hard mining precious finds
Refilling weekly shopping cart
To wait in endless lines.

Or at the new Flea Market lot…
Now there's some serious junk!
High-fashion gunk that might be hot
Or not….goes in the trunk.

The Congressman re-clears his throat
A mighty mass of phlegm.
Pulls out some scribble he just wrote
No one would call a gem.

  I'm <u>so</u> proud to be standing here
  At our new Farkwart Bridge.
  Could someone, please, get me a beer?
  I think I need a smidge.

Yes, folks, it is a joyous day
A gift straight from my heart
To mold this from some lump of clay
Into sleek work of art.

Some might call this a hunk of steel
As they've sat, scratched, and mulled.
They don't know all the deals I wheeled
The rings of strings I pulled.

But here's the Bridge to Nowhere Ridge
A bridge 'cross NoChance Creek
As pretty as your grammaw's fridge
Before it starts to wreak.

I know you all must be so proud…
Heard couple of you cough…
I'll take some questions from the crowd
But then I must be off.

    Yes, Mr. Farkwart, tell me why
    The bridge beams have no paint.
They're "stainless", Son, that would imply
Those beams will never taint.

    Sir, was it hard to get this passed
    With others wanting funds?
It was.  But I pushed hard and fast
Won favors by the tons.

Have time for one more question, guys
Yes, You….wife-beater shirt…
        A Bridge to Nowhere…?  Was that wise…?
        There's nothing there but dirt!

(whispers)
>    Pssst…Hey, McGrotch…stop lingerin'
>    Were s'posed to screen this crowd.
>    How did you let that Ringer in?
>    Especially one so loud!

>       Were s'posed to call that other dude
>       The <u>stained</u> wife-beater shirt!!
>       The stained dude had been thoroughly clued
>       Serve softball Q to blurt.

(back at microphone)
>    Yes sir….the Bridge…the Bridge you ask?
>    A bridge that's sorely needed.
>    This complex engineering task
>    A need that now's been heeded.

>       But what's it for?  What will we gain?
>       There's nothing over there.
>       And then you made the thing 4-lane
>       Just want to get things square.

>    There was no way to cross the creek
>    Unless you like to swim
>    <u>You</u> may be some prized swimming geek
>    But what 'bout him, him, him?

>    No, this is something that we need.
>    The project never slowed.
>    Besides, it's built to handle speed
>    It's built to carry load.

>       There's nothing on that other side
>       'Cept swamp, and mud, and rocks
>       And smells like a full species died
>       Of some strange Nowhere Pox.

Meanwhile, McGrotch cuts off the beer
The crowd now's getting tense.
The beer's made them forget their fear
They start to climb the fence.

The late-arriving cocktail dogs
Are starting to get launched
They find their way into the bogs
And make that wetland raunched.

Then ducks appear from near and far
To dine on these cold dogs
Looks like could be the start of war….
Dog-war 'tween ducks and frogs.

The crowd is struck by this duck scene
Must be 3 thousand ducks
The most ducks that they'd ever seen…
"They're crapping on our trucks!!"

They run for cover in their cabs
Then quickly hit the gas
So who will pay for car-wash tabs
To clean this defiled mess?

The parking lot's an empty lot
In 'bout 3 blinks of eye
With trucks adorned in polka-dot
From peltings from the sky.

McGrotch, with jaw dropped to his crotch,
Still thinking he's a goner
Looks at the trucks besmeared in blotch
And glances at Hizzoner.

But Farkwart smiles and walks away
"Oh my, this came out well.
How fortunate…that timely spray
Made all those hayseeds yell."

He boards his ride, this time a Benz
And crosses his new bridge
He's got a date with Hunter friends
O'er there at Nowhere Ridge.

Got work to do….the good-fun kind
May even bust some buns.
Improving their duck-hunting blind
With those "excess" bridge funds

# Texas Back-scratch Poker

The Fat Cat Board arrives at Six
Aboard their private planes
With background riffs and licks from Bix
They park it on their brains.

The caviar and French Champagne
Are what these Cats expect
Imported Angel fish from Spain
The Chairman's wife had spec'ed

Give brand new meaning to "high stakes"
Drink 21-year scotch
Goes well with thick aged New York steaks
Top shelf…who's gonna watch?

High rollers who make funny sounds
Feet seldom touch real ground
They manage by <u>not</u> walking 'round
They manage to gain pounds.

The dealer pulls a brand new deck
Deals out… one Up, one Down
Each player turns and cranes his neck
Checks hands of fellow clown.

And then take quick peeks at their hole
Slap on a poker face
Such face as gruesome as a troll
Could almost scare a vase.

Pretenders to be serious
But most, of course, are not
You'd think they were delirious
Between loud blows of snot.

Keep cards secure, hide close to vest
Show shifty eyes, slid sly
To keep close eye on every guest
But they're not quite sure why.

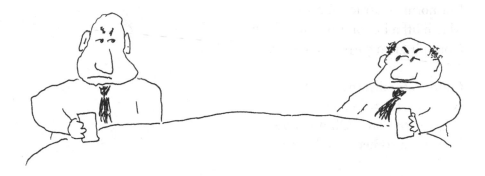

The Back-scratch Poker game begins
The worst up-card Cat starts
Gets palm off of his multi-chins
Sneaks out a couple farts

Can trade a Card with one Board Bud
But first must scratch his back.
Without inflicting creepy crud
From some dumb cheese spread snack.

The Scratchee can then make the trade
If back scratch strokes don't stall
If feels as good as getting laid
As best he can recall.

But these Joes are back scratching pro's
They know scratch-otomy
Trained under Moes whose talent shows
Since their lobotomy.

The CEO must now decide
Since he is on the Button
To bet, to sweat, or let it ride
Or show his skill at sluttin'

Now anyone can challenge him
But norm – just let him win
May bluff a bet on some weird whim
Commit grim corporate sin.

Quite naturally, the CFO
Is Banker for the game
Allowed to Play?  Oh no.  Lord, no.
They need someone to blame.

As Banker, he must dole out chips
To these dukes of skyscrapers
The wanker who runs out of chips
Must cut up little papers.

    Old Thumpnard raises 20 chips
    But all think it's a bluff
    Can tell Bluff when Thump's forehead drips
    And perspir-stains his cuff.

    They're all high masters of the bluff
    Bluffed so much in the past
    One Cat once bluffed that he liked snuff
    Stuff started flying fast.

Backscratch goes till each back's been scratched
And best hand wins the pot
If pot's too small, more funds get snatched
The Bank forks what he's got

If any Cat objects to this
He's kindly asked to leave
The game returns to one of bliss
Of normal tricks up sleeve.

The Outsiders, called Stockholders
Are not allowed to play
Can whine and pout, throw rock-boulders
But won't help lengthen stay.

Can pray…that these strays play things right
Maybe prayers will be heard
Could be the Sun will shine at night
Could see a sharp-dressed nerd.

They're shuffled out the Poker room
And told "have a nice day"
Take poached reports of Anti-gloom
And please come back next May!

The Chairman, at some point mid-game
Gets up…stares out the glass
Then drifts off in some fog of maim
And mows his ass of grass

May count his losings, just for laughs
But hardly makes a diff
May reminisce of last year's gaffes
Or next year's smurfs he'll stiff

He may spinoff a sidebar game
To keep from getting bored
For special scratching without shame
Could get a tad untoward.

If all these Members have bad hands
If not one lousy pair
The rule says that the pot just stands
And no one gets a share

But these cats…they don't give a rip
Don't follow that dumb rule
Give this script a symbolic flip
That rule can go eat stool.

And in the end, all Fat Cats win
With wallets packed with dough
Plus scratchwork that excites the skin
And blankets of new snow

Each Fat Cat leaves a winner, but
Each Cat leaves as a loser.
May not have gotten thinner, but
Got chance to be a boozer.

Did any Substance come from this
Besides this wallet pad?
Decisions beyond when to piss…
E'en if those calls were bad?

Don't know what they deliberate
'Cept giving selves some bumps
Don't know if they'd defibrillate
If some poor Fat Cat slumps.

Then off they go, back whence they came
Go back from firsts to noneths
Well satisfied from this strange game
Will be back in 3 months.

# The President's Magic Ring

The morning sun peeks from old oaks
The back lawn comes alive
A distant sound of pond frog croaks
Drone bees in search of hive.

He loves to take these post-dawn strolls
One moment of sheer peace.
Away from gurgling insta-polls
Debate who's next to fleece.

What's that?  A sparkling little speck
'Spects someone lost a dime
Bends over, nearly strains his neck
Then pulls it from the grime.

A ring?  A ring?  What's with this thing?
Old 'nuff to be James Polk's
I wonder what this ring would bring
From Antique Roadshow folks.

He cleans it with embroidered hanky
Muddies up Prez seal.
The ring's still looking pretty skanky
Has a grimy feel.

Then notices an inscribed writ:
"The Wearer has 3 wishes
Least one must truly benefit
Constituents with riches

"Or All the Wishes won't sustain."
He thinks he gets the drill.
One wish must show a culture gain
Or all 3 will be nil.

He looks around.  Is this a hoax?
A Candid Camera bit?
First Lady likes to play these jokes
Which make me look the twit.

Decides to give this ring a go
Thinks:  So what?  What's the harm?
If prank, will make a darn good show.
Had better show some charm.

He slips it on.  Wish Number One.
Let's have:  <u>Health Care for All.</u>
Then POOF !!  Sees smoke.  Feels one slight stun.
And wonders:  Is that all?

But magically, the Wish comes true.
A wave from sea to sea.
Each citizen, illegals too
Have health coverage for free.

No more the dumb deductible
The Out-of-pocket Max
The walls so indestructible
To just clear up the facts.

The wrangling with insurance firms
The endless stream of forms.
The haggling over payment terms
The hapless "health reforms".

Debates about who's gonna pay
And who will get free rides
The bill for endless hosp'tal stay
For mommas who aren't brides.

Insurance for the un-insured
Who choose 'tween food and pills
Bifocals for the multi-blurred
Who can't decipher bills.

Viagras at the Quickie Mart
Dispensed at vend machines.
New baby boom could may well start
Who knows… might spike 'mong teens.

Free wheelchairs for folks with sore feet
Free CAT scans for all bumps
Free salves for sharp pains up their seat
Cuz no one likes sore rumps.

Free dentistry for every mouth
Help those who've never brushed
Decayed mouths from the rural south
Whose gums have gotten sloshed.

But soon, the ominous clouds arrive.
The lines start getting long.
Seems no one thought there'd be deprive
The system seemed so strong…?

Ms. Blumbar had a heart attack
But told to take a Number
Will she end up flat on her back…
Route to eternal slumber?

Installed those theme park gate corrals
For waits at Smarknard Clinic.
For free checks of your genitals
Their MD's such a cynic.

Turns out, it's now a numbers game
Docs paid by volume through.
Then wait to see if their checks came
Through all the red-tape goo.

Bill Smith came for an allergy shot
But got in the wrong line.
The surgery found no heart clot
Found all his knots benign.

The dentists stopped the fillings, bridge
To root canals?  Bye Bye
Put your teeth pictures on your fridge
Mass dentures on the fly.

The good Docs head for Hilton Head
Forced by new drop in passion.
New home, new boat, new luxo-sled
New insight now to cash-in.

Which makes the long lines longer now
Prez poll stats start to tank.
Must be ways to unsank…but how?
The rancor's gotten rank.

Looks at the Ring that's bruised his skin
Looks like we're 0 for 1.
Next wish had better be a win
Might have to learn to run.

The Quality of Education
Must be great for each.
The future key to our great nation
Rests in how we teach.

Must beautify the dumpy schools
Pay every teacher more
Free college, even for the fools
Raise every grade and score.

Then, POOF !!  Schools get a lift of face
A shot of fresh Botox.
New place for all new wastes-of-space
Grew space for larger clocks.

Each teacher gets a 10-K pop
And 10 more if they're great
But all will get this over-top
This Op is all self-rate.

All kids now get a college grant
Can pick their school of choice
No matter if they can or can't
Read books, or put down toys.

But soon, the clouds roll in once more
Some unplanned zags and zigs.
The deadbeats who hated school before
Still hate it in new digs.

Bad teachers have not got un-bad
Just cuz they got more bread.
Sad programs have not got un-sad
Just cuz they got more lead.

The college classes add deadload
New ranks of lack-of-clue
Who don't want to be on this road
Or list of Who's-Not-Who.

Endowments now have shriveled up
Say donors: What's the point?
The Excellence has given up
There's sniveling in this joint.

A mediocrity's took hold
In finest colleges
With windows broke, in Halls of Mold
And no mold-ologists.

Hard-working students are now bummed
As standards slip and slide.
Their college pride's been soundly drummed
The glum of unrolled tide.

Perhaps Prez wishes were naïve.
They sounded good in theory.
May've bit off more than he could heave
When things seemed much more cheery.

Maybe best let these Wishes die?
Or will things come around?
Cannot further unzip my fly
My blue chip stock has drowned.

Guess if I make one more bad call
Won't matter anyway
Guess I'll go 'head and play this ball
And just plain swing away.

Stop Energy Dependence on
Those creep-skies from Mid East.
Will have to pay some penance on
Our oil consumption feast.

Then POOF !!  A hushed new quiet comes
Like Prez turned down the sound.
Or someone muffled down the drums
That rumbled 'cross the ground.

He looks around, surprised to see
All cars and trucks are gone.
Those users of such energy
Those nasty beasts of brawn.

No more the guzzling SUV's
No more the Station wagon
No more machines in need of grease
No need for license taggin'.

Replaced all cars with bikes and trikes
And quikes replaced the trucks
Replaced long road trips with short hikes
And bike rides just for yuks.

And gone are all electric lights…
Was this part of the bargain?
Be packin' candles late at night
I guess we won't be parkin'.

The washers and the dishwashers
Are dead in their own waters.
Will miss sounds from those grit sloshers
Give scrub brush to the daughters.

Restrooms are out, outhouses in.
Much water to be saved.
Six trillion flushes – such a sin
Just takes all getting braved.

His Air Force One turned "Road Force Ten"
A tandem 10-speed bike
With Pope-mobile bubble skin
To guard 'gainst Prez dislike.

The Secretary – Energy
Is now an Amish deacon
Will soon rein in his ministry
And handle people freakin'.

But this wish has achieved its goal
Oil imports crash to zip.
Don't even burn all that much coal
They found the switch to flip.

It's solved the global warming scare
It's purged the greenhouse gas
Folks started eating their meat Rare
Got on mule, got off ass.

They started to get exercise
With bodies not quite ready.
No longer eating jumbo fries
Still fat/obese, but steady.

That's it.  It seems that's all it took:
Step back 200 years.
Turn off the tube, pick up the book
Thank God, can still get beers.

So all 3 wishes get to stand
The Prez seems sorta glad.
Tries to squeeze that Ring off his hand
But must have gotten clad.

# The Economic Crisis Debrief

A hush falls 'cross this anxious crowd
Reporters, Cross pens drawn
Expecting pundits to get loud
Critiquing when they've gone.

The Secretary Treasury
Takes podium, stage right.
His staff guys are still measuring
Untangling this plight.

Good morning, Friends.  The trends look grim.
We're now amending mends.
The hedge fund meltdown failed to swim
Dismantled congress cleanse.

The central bank disliquidate
Destabilize rank angst
Then default refault replicate
Receded from the shankst.

Illiquid credit market moons
Uncertain dry froon drapes
Pay tax deferred 5-year balloons
For loon-refractive tapes.

We must trust furlong crays of crust
De-under-regulate
And not discuss the gust disgust
Not dust de-speculate.

The Fed Chief then appears stage left.
Lugs in a book of notes.
A book of legendary heft.
To help point out the goats.

　　　Good morning, All.  Our plane's gone stall.
　　　We need to get back flyin'
　　　Our cash box's gone from tall to small
　　　Need something else be tryin'.

　　　The Secretary makes good points
　　　A tighter grip past-due
　　　The mark-to-market point disjoints
　　　Is apt to next ensue.

　　　Collateralizing lending trend
　　　Unmitigated loss
　　　Deteriorating retail spend
　　　That spurs too much ginned gloss.

　　　Those under-blundered balance sheets
　　　Of public private throng
　　　Deplete more tyrus callous cleats
　　　Beat mortgage cats reclong.

You're right.  Infractions gone amok.
Must hold their feet to fire
Tri-party repo stuffage stuck
Redeem, refloat, rewire.

Rix raven wristband reed reweave
To find trix vantage green
Not forging fur bank lean quiz heave
Their care quart burfiss bean  (ha ha)

That's funny.  But get serious.
The road must go through Trent.
To balance Bixford, curious
That's not what Bill Gates meant.

A resolution cap accord
Re-flexxing spiral gloof
Perplexing bailout blox untoward
Inspecting day fraud floof.

Dux fraculate dim free zan slotch
Botch culminate crod klimm
Then trim beskim the frankle splotch
Come crankle despot dim.

Exactly, I've said all along
But no one seems to listen
Restatulate!  Restatulate!!
Greeb bommit flommit flissen.

Dismantle all these comvolt klarbs
Far barb dix donut derd
Malfunk truncated aardvark harbs
Destunk on conant curd.

It's not as simple as you say
Transfaction comes in play
Deshlunk crass Maynard oxy-clay
Can frax el stooge mis-may.

I'm sorry... but our time is done.
I thank our 2 fine guests
Last questions...?  My, I guess there's none
Ha, ha... the Defense rests.

# Shake Stamps

Debate fights have gone on for weeks
Much longer than they need
The search for ways to get li'l squeaks
To pique their need to read.

Their reading comprehension scores
To say the least, have slipped.
They've dropped below the floor's subfloors
Fell in some sorta crypt.

But how on earth to turn this tide
That nearly swamped the boat?
What subsidy has not been tried?
What prop-up trick to float?

Then Nuxford dreamed a scheme with hooks
A thought he dubbed:  Shake Stamps.
Free chocolate shakes for teen-bought books
No chocolate shakes for Gramps.

They did the Math.  Would cost ten bil
To have these kids swill shakes.
The more they read, the more they fill
Their guts with pre-fab aches.

The Stamps can only be redeemed
At first-class choc shake bars.
At places where each shake's whip-creamed
Might touch off choc shake wars.

Post launch, all seems to be on-course
Shakes pouring in the paunch.
And books are moving out the doors
Nux' Stamp plan's looking staunch.

But kids start getting Super-size
They shop in chubby aisles.
Been drinking shakes with sides of fries
And now've got case of piles.

The chocolate's popped up acne sprouts
With heads of black and white.
And dreads of Rudolph red-nose snouts
Put out a frightful sight.

Test scores have not gone up a lick
Or in this case…a slurp.
Must be the books have found some creek
Sunk under globs of glurp.

Vanilla makers' picket lines
Gripe:  This is so Unfair!
Hold <u>Flavor Discrimination</u> signs
They want their fair shake share.

Then Magazines say: We're like books
Our tabloids help kids read.
Can't judge book covers by their looks
Our breed read's built for speed.

The Mags meet with the 'Nilla gang
Decide to join at hip.
Not let this gross injustice hang
Want their own trough to sip.

Magilla partners take their case
Upstairs on Capitol Hill.
And lobby the whole freaking place
To any who'd stand still.

What shake payola may've gone down?
Free malt shop trips for two?
Or passes down to Tastee Town
To sample brew of moo?

Soon Congress passed Shakes Stamps Rev Two
And doubled Shake Stamp funds.
Provisions now for you-know-who
And added: shakes for nuns.

No movement still in Reading score
Despite the glut of shakes.
But <u>did</u> find nuns were reading more
Between their vespers breaks.

The Dentist's working overtime
The staff's behind on billings
They're cleaning out the Silver mine
To whip up paste for fillings.

Has not been so much drilling done
Since those yon days of Chunnel.
Unwilling, filling-spitting done
Into that dentoid funnel.

Soon, bars start subbing ice cream waste
For top-shelf fresh ice cream.
Shakes don't taste like they used to taste…
This flavored shaving cream.

Investigation's on full-tilt
No way this silt can wait.
Can't give our Shake Stamps plan this jilt
Can't have a Shake-R-Gate.

A couple fines, the Willful kind…
Ignoring Shake Stamp rules
To fools who never had been fined
Remand to Ice Cream schools.

Then suddenly in Omaha
The first outbreak occurs
Then quickly spreads to Wichita
So fast… the picture blurs.

The Brain-freeze epidemic hits
Strikes most kids within days.
It frosts up all their teeny wits
And makes their eyeballs glaze.

The kids become decorticate
Like weasels in the night.
An icy brain-wave tourniquet
That turned their jaundice white.

The frantic parents want to know:
What's in these crazy shakes?
What makes these shakes flow head-to-toe
To give our kids freeze-quakes.

The best Docs from across the land
Converge to troubleshoot.
Fast answers are what moms demand
"Stop all shakes," they conclude.

"The hypo-thermal overload
Transferred on such small nugget
Contracts the oblongata node
That basically says: Awww, frugget."

So Congress meets to pour out whine:
How can this get undone?
To cut this Stamp Act from the vine
To help our kids un-stun.

But try, try, retry as they might...
They can't undo this craze.
They can't un-fly the chocolate kite.
They can't unlight the blaze.

The Shake Stamp Law is too darn tight
To fend 'gainst rewrite fears.
Might be a chance to get it right
In 8 to 13 years.

Meanwhile, the Reading scores have slid
A program cold-to-trot.
Where have all those new books been hid?
A question well forgot.

# Bums' Rights

A march of Bums on city square
Has got town folk disturbed.
Dressed up in finest bumber wear
And sounding quite perturbed:

> We Bum feel that we have the Right
> To smell bad as we wish.
> Not deal with all your high-crust spite
> Cuz our class wreaks of fish.

> It's more than just this Right to Stench
> Our Bill of Right to swill.
> Conditions of the town's park bench
> Have trenched.  Gone straight down hill.

> Think of those benches as <u>our</u> homes.
> All need a fresh re-plane.
> Be nice if you'd install some domes
> To keep off sleet and rain.

> There's no one who protects our Rights
> Get treated like some crook.
> Like our rights to go start some fights
> If dude gives me a look.

> That <u>look</u> is what should be a crime.
> Comes off so mean, so sleazy.
> Those lookers need to do hard time
> Don't let them off so easy.

We used to find old cigar nubs
That some old rich guy tossed.
Now some shmoe sweeps outside the pubs
<u>That</u> really makes us cross.

They now won't let us wear that card
That says "Will Work for Food."
Just cuz we've never cleaned a yard
Nor ever seen un-stewed.

Pan-handling's part of history
American tradition.
You guys think it's some mystery
Should bathe out your suspicion

Cuz handling pans, a passed-down Art
Requires a fine technique.
Can burp.  But must not sneak a fart…
Might cause a Mark to freak.

We should be a Protected Class
Who choose to rest on can.
A class that loves to sleep on grass
Or smoke grass when we can.

A lifestyle choice of Anti-poise
Whose problem's been deferred
We want a voice for our white noise
We want our noise box heard.

Our founding fathers wrote about
Pursuit of Happiness.
We're happy when we're hanging out
Without your work-day stress.

Want to pursue our right to crash,
Pursue right to malinger.
Without you Workies talking trash
And flashing us your finger.

Just want respect from you Un-Bum
To stop your laughing wink
We see your noses that you thumb
Just cuz our armpits stink.

Demand we get free Undershirt
Free access to the Laundry.
Oh never mind… can live with dirt
Would be too much a quandary.

Want price caps on cheap types of wine
No more than half a buck.
For bummage who prefer to dine
On scraps of lamb or duck.

Soup kitchens need some better soup
We're sick of Chicken Rice.
With spice made out of chicken poop
Recycled once or twice.

How 'bout Beef Veggie Demi-glazed?
How 'bout some Lobster Bisque?
Some soup that has some real soup taste
Less salmonella risk.

In dumpster dives, we Bum compete
But venue choice is slim-picks
Still, this is one most skillful feat
Should be in the Olympics.

McSlump arrived and gloved his fists
At Pistmann Deli's dump.
Did somersault with 2 nice twists
Sweet entry on his rump.

Degree of difficulty:  3
An 8-point judge's score.
Dug deep to find a wedge of brie
That gave him 2 points more.

Our dumpster dives are all 'bout form
I've seen Bums look like swans
Not make a splash in raging storm
Clean as them Porta-johns.

We used to use discarded News
As basically our blanket.
Newspapers are now last year's news
Decided just to yank it.

We're now forced to use Xerox sheets
But they're so gosh-darn short.
They barely cover up our feets
So full of planters warts.

      More public restrooms on each street
      To help clean up gross alleys
      Stamp out the "Patrons Only" sheets
      In windows of most galleys.

      Especially for female bums
      Who face some tougher issues.
      Whose needs go far beyond us chums…
      Who seem to need them tissues.

You say:  Hey, let's clean up this town
Let's clean up downtown streets.
Go start by taking billboards down
And lockup stock-trade cheats.

Don't need to pick on our poor crowd
Our swarms will do no harms.
Arrest kids with bass turned-up loud
Or cars with armed alarms.

Prefer to be called <u>Workophobes</u>
Instead of tag line "Bum".
Please don't say we're those guys in robes
Would not hang with that scum.

We're Workophobes.  Get that down pat.
We're people.  Just don't work.
And so what?  So, what's wrong with that?
Wipe smirk.  Go back to work.

# The Failure of the Goat

He looks much thinner every day
Reduced to bag of bones.
Thin goatee that's been turning gray
Same's true of his goat clones.

The rich bluegrass that had sustained
This herd of mangy goat
Is almost gone cuz it's not rained
Since time of last year's vote.

His friends – the bugs and grasshoppers
The squirmy worms who've turned.
They love these funny grass-chompers
But now've become concerned.

    What will become of our dear friend?
    Will they just wither 'way?
    Could Mother Nature's plan intend
    To render goats in clay?

They love the goat's cool bedroom eyes
Love goat's smooth Latin dance.
But mostly how goats fertilize
The island's grass and plants

Seem to dispel more than they eat
Must be some sorta catch.
But makes the grass patch green and sweet…
Well… sweet may be a stretch.

The beetles shake their heads, decry:
"Why don't they just eat Rye?
Seems like goats should give rye a try,
Would rather rye than die."

But goats remember years ago
When Jack Goat ate fresh rye.
His show looked like Bellagio
With fluids flowing high.

So they've been gun shy of the rye
No one wants Jack replay.
Meanwhile, the puzzled flock of fly
Say: "What be our next play?"

Do we wish to help goats succeed
Or hope that they should ail?
Be on the side to save this breed
Or speed the path to fail?

Cuz if those goats start eating rye
Could eat us from our home.
They'll snarf the rye that we rely
So we don't constant roam.

But if these old goats up and croak
Gone will be their trip-trap
We'll miss the way they crack a joke
We'll lose their nutri-crap.

"A crisis in our own backyard.
Poor kids who ought be shaved."
The Mantis started praying hard:
Should these 4-legs be saved?

The Caterpillars say:  Hell no!
Just let them billies starve.
Else they'll find every blade that grows
And show how well they carve.

Why let these gangly goofs succeed?
They're such a bunch of dufes.
No tellin' where this path will lead
For these dumb beasts with hoofs.

But swarms of Lady bugs then spoke:
You squirmers are plain nuts.
Been breathing too much swamp grass smoke
Brought out your sense of klutz.

Admit it... you don't like the Goat
You've never liked the Goat.
All <u>you</u> care 'bout is your own boat
As you go stuff your throat.

Goats've lived here for a thousand years
And look... we've all survived.
You're stirring up unfounded fears
With fresh drears you've contrived.

Perhaps <u>you</u> need to sacrifice
Tight-up your 50 belts
Have altruism rechecked twice
See if your iced-heart melts.

Remember that we <u>need</u> the goats
For all their drops and squirt
Look how it's helped those tall wild oats
If gone... we'll feel the hurt.

Okay, so short-term, we may see
Less fertilizer drops
Less plops from tree to shining tree
May wimpify some crops

But listen… we can solve this stuff
How to enrich our fields.
Our ingenuity is tough
Be 'mazed at what it yields.

Most goats are garbage-eating fiends
Chomp anything that grows.
Get so fat that it hurts their knees
They're worse than those danged crows.

Let's just let Nature take its course
Like Food chain's managed 'fore.
Let's not let Goats start Insect Wars…
Been through that mess before.

Besides, how will you get the Goat
To want to eat the rye?
Won't want to stand in their own moat
That's full of rye grass pie.

We'll mix rye with remaining blue
Those goats will hardly know.
Get systems to adjust to new
Without the grand spew show.

The other insects jumped on board
On side to save goat breed
Momentum's spreading 'mong the horde
Just like a patch of weed.

The Caterpillars feel the pinch
The stinging barbs of greed
Caught up inside this insect winch
Impending frenzy feed.

How 'bout we spout a compromise…
How would y'all feel 'bout that?
A plan set up so no goat dies
But no goat gets too fat.

A diet?  Goat on diet plan?
Get them to count their carbs?
Will that fly with the whole goat clan?
Can almost hear goat barbs.

Perhaps when goats all realize
We insects saved their skin
They might accept the compromise.
(Or we will do them in.)

Debate continued through the night
At end, both sides agreed
A well-thought plan with details tight
That Lady Bugs would lead.

So every night, as goat breed slept
The bugs would meet the need
Each species would get quite adept
At their appointed deed.

And soon the rye was mixed with blue
Looked like the real deal.
Gave off a sparkling teal hue
Still had the nice soft feel.

The goats then ate this grassy mix
And did not know the diff.
'Cept seemed to have a few more kicks
And made their hind leg stiff.

The bugs kept moving more and more
Till rye mix was 'bout half
And never heard a stomach roar
A growl, a grunt, a laugh.

Success.  Adapted to the rye
Ensuring they'd endure
No more the fear of wither, die
Together, worked the cure.

Then later at a Council meet
Explained all to the Goat
How bugs pulled off this awesome feat
Of this mass rye grass tote.

The goats shocked, stupefied, surprised...
How could we not have known?
How could we not have just surmised
That something strange was goin'?

The Goat Herd thanks you for your care
You saved us from demise.
We're even growing back our hair
Restarted telling lies.

Oh, one more thing. We must insist
You goats stay on a diet.
Control your intake... don't get pissed
It's discipline... just try it.

You bet. We've learned our lesson now.
Not eat like we're like pigs.
Must think about kids future chow
And think about your digs.

And so, the Goats left with their vow
But soon fell off the wagon
Back emulating Mister Cow
Their tummies started saggin'.

What's up with this? Is this some diss?
You're back to your old tricks?
Our 'greement's just got thrown in piss
And makes a stinky mix.

Well, yes, we tried. We surely tried.
We tried to stay on diet.
I'd even yell, and scold, and chide
But mostly told to fly it.

Cuz we're hard-programmed just to eat
Seems something we can't change.
I'm sorry.  But we cannot meet
Our vows…we must estrange.

    We're sorry, too.  Had hoped this'd work
    But now must do Plan B.
    Those wasps there… can you see them lurk…
    There lurking by the tree?

    I'm 'fraid tonight they'll start to sting
    Each fat slob, obese goat
    Will bring on some gross nausea-thing
    And help dispel their bloat.

    Will leave the nice trim goats alone
    The ones who've stayed the course.
    Who've kept goat bodies in fine tone
    Look like a tiny horse.

And so the Balance then returns
'Mong Island bugs and beasts
With new lush grasses, oats, and ferns
For disciplined new feasts.

# Bye Gurdy

Oooh, toodle-loo to Gurdy Sears
It's time to say good-bye.
Oh my, has it been 40 years?
Aaah, sigh, the time does fly.

Ole Gurdy's desk was by the stairs
She took her break at nine.
She's kind.  She never put on airs.
I never heard her whine.

She'd cry and die vicariously
With each co-worker plight.
No sad song felt disparately
Kept Kleenex right in sight.

I guess I'd say we'll miss that girl
But not sure what she does.
She made her calculator swirl.
Her keyboard was a-buzz.

She rarely took on extra load
There'd be some veiled threat.
Of stopped-up pipes that backwash flowed
For time tables not met.

Each year review a solid "Met"
No cheers, no tears, no sneers.
No understanding <u>what</u> she met…
Who knows what throes she steers.

She could have been a whole lot more
Or whole lot less, we'd guess.
Would rarely open up her store
To show what she'd repress.

Her in-box was an empty bin.
She thinned her in-box fast
Or maybe nothing's coming in…
Oh well, that die's been cast.

Bureaucracy takes one deft touch
To file all red tape right
To paw through drudge, old fudge, and such
Unsmudged with drops of Sprite.

The paperwork and protocol
Must be done with precision.
There's no such thing as "judgment call"…
No, not in this religion.

And Gurdy…she knew all the rules
Or we assume she knew.
Learned from old secretary pools
Way back in '72.

She always came through in the clutch
If "clutch" is what you'd call it.
Her office didn't clutch too much
Except when someone bought it.

Knows where they've placed the buried bods
Helped bury some herself.
Can point out all the married clods
Who now rest on some shelf.

A civil servant 40 years…
Or 41, who counts?
A journey full of tactile veers
While fearing each announce.

Just can't replace experience
She had her job down pat.
She had a certain purience
In doing daily scat.

A countdown calendar she kept
And X'ed off days four years.
She'd dreamed of X's as she slept
Leapt up as R-day nears.

And then her big day finally came…
Surprising, little cheer.
New future without any aim…
Not like there's been aim here.

How will we get by without Gurd?
Things just won't be the same.
What will we miss that we've not heard
That kept us in some game?

So who will take up the baton?
What's the baton to take?
As she gets off, who will get on?
What mess-ups won't she make?

What Gurdy tasks might fall through cracks?
And, if so, where'll they go?
To Office Limbo, via fax
Unknowable to know.

# The 10 trillion cubic foot hole

He'd dug a hole in his backyard
Which measured 1-foot square.
Can't recall if that ground was hard
Or if that grass was bare.

Or what he started digging for…?
Was it to plant some plant?
Keep bees away from his back door?
Think back…alas, he can't.

But clearly did not fill it back
So it remained a cleft.
Tomorrow, he'd go back, repack
And finish what he left.

Had noticed that small terns would swim
"Oh isn't that so sweet!"
Go give the hole a little trim
To give room to excrete.

He carved the Hole, now 3-feet square
And dug it 2-feet deep
So birds could come from everywhere…
He'd hear chirps in his sleep.

If we made this hole 10-feet square
The ducks would see this pond
Adorn our backyard with such flair
With serenade so fond.

Oh ducks would come, and geese would come
But small birds flew away.
The yard was anything but mum
Quack-honk-honk-gonk all day.

He made the pond a skosh more wide
By now it filled his yard.
His watchful neighbor finally cried,
"I'd like a pond, too, Pard."

Expanded his pond's ruddy reach
While anxious neighbors stared.
"We want some of this budding beach."
Got out their trenching ware.

Soon neighbor kids had hole to swim
New spot to beat the heat.
Jump in and swim, on any whim
Deodorize your feet.

A pool (of sorts) for the whole town
Where all could take quick dips.
They'd quip:  this could unfrown a clown.
They'd cancel Disney trips.

But skeeters liked the pond, as well
And chowed-down on the runts.
With bites so big, they'd ooze and swell
Produce runt growls and grunts.

Li'l Jake had noticed little stones
On bottom of this lake.
"A gravel pit!"  his father groans
"Stones ready for the take."

Next, Acme Gravel digs through muck
And sure enough…found clones.
Brings backhoe, dozer, loader, truck
To mine this glut of stones.

And shortly the town's swimming swamp
Became an open pit.
No more a pool where rug rats romp.
Now backhoes that won't quit.

Demolished small homes in their path
And flattened all their hampers.
Created this town's Stones of Wrath.
Grew new unhappy campers.

    There's money in those tiny rocks.
    It might unbox our town.
    Need something to unlock our stocks
    And <u>this</u> might be the crown.

So dig and dig and dig they did.
Mined nine buzillion stone.
Discovered voids that had been hid
'Neath dirt lids overgrown.

    We 'ventually must fill this in…
    But right now, not to worry.
    Let's peel back one more layer o' skin
    Keep pumping all that slurry.

And when they thought they'd bottomed out
And sieved out all last stones
And scooped out every ounce of grout
That's when they found the Bones.

"Jurassic Age," the expert said
Conglomma-saurus leg.
Let's call this dino:  Uncle Fred
Try find his dead mate, Meg.

A shalely hole for paleos
With tons of earth pre-dug.
Now they won't muddy-up their clothes
To find old bones and bugs.

More excavating work ahead
Wide out this gulf a smidge
Now 2 miles wide from foot to head
One mile drop from its ridge.

But after digging, Diggers found
Old Freddie had no mate.
Not till they'd unearthed mounds of ground
And hauled it by the crate.

Made token starts to cart backfill
But could not get 'nuff psyched.
Just could not muster up the will
For task so much disliked.

Then someone saw an oily spot
'Round just behind the Crusher.
They noticed that the ground felt hot:
"I think we've got a Gusher!"

    A gusher...huh?  In this abyss?
    Need drill a little deeper?
    Are we prepared to go through this
    To chase a little weeper?

They drilled and dug to find some oil
But no oil was t'be found.
Turned out was crankcase overboil
That splotched out on the ground.

But now, geologists had shown
In their small make-shift lab
At base inside of ancient stone
Atop a pre-cam slab…

    Will need to drill down 1 more mile
    Just found a vein of coal.
    Has Btu's plum off the dial
    Near bottom of this bowl.

They hired more trucks to haul the spill
Ran 24 and 7.
Then dumped it in some stretched landfill
A mound halfway to heaven.

    Some cried:  Let's backfill.  Backfill now.
    Before we're in too deep.
    Before we simply forget how.
    Before we lose more sleep.

The diggers thought of this as noise
Noise needing drowning out
They hosed them down, while keeping poise
"Stay course.  Not horse about."

Of course that course was pointing down
A big and bigger crater.
That now engulfed the next small town
With one queued up for later.

The children got a wee bit scared
Have never seen such gap.
Stay back from where the rim is flared
Don't lose your new ballcap.

Erosion helps the hole grow more
To rhythms of the rain.
Folks wonder: Will they find the floor
Before they reach Bahrain?

Burns up 10 gallons diesel fuel
To get truck up these ramps
Two minutes for Gramps' glob of drool
To spray the bottom camps.

So here it is:  a vast devoid
That's 6 miles long, 6 wide
And 2 miles deep formed trapezoid
A landscape fairly fried.

It's got too big to ever fill
That's not stopped dig of stone
Guess they'll just dig until they kill
Last shovel that they own.

They've made Big Hole a tourist spot
Charge mere 10 bucks a head.
Guests marvel at how big it's got
And how big it may get.

# Mars Cars

"Say what??" he screams at top of voice.
"You surely must be kidding.
Ain't no job for goof-boys with toys
Whose skill range stops at spitting."

No matter. This decision's done.
New Lead team for Mars Cars
Who'll inject some new kind of fun
Like exploding cigars.

Poor Meldnut's gonna get the boot.
Mars' next ex-President
With Feds deciding to permute
This group who can't pay rent.

Seems Meld did not go far enough
To meet Fed's expectation.
Quite certain wasn't czar enough
To head off conflagration.

But now Feds brought in brand new chief
Who promised not to jerk us.
Ex-ringmaster and part-time thief
Who came from Durfbird's Circus.

Brought cirque performers to key slots
Cat-tamers tracked details.
The Jugglers managed storage lots
Brought Clowns in to run Sales.

The Peanut vendors run Finance
Key cash skills – theirs to brag.
Shook many wallets out guests' pants
To pay 8 bucks a bag.

The guys that shoveled creature poop
Will be Mars Engineers.
Their useful skills in how to scoop
Will help design new gears.

Trapezers run assembly lines
Trick riders run road tests
The Freak show hucksters draw designs
That everyone detests.

Designed the latest front-end steel
Based on Beard Lady's beard.
Designed a satin steering wheel
No clue on how car's steered.

Hard Head, the Human Cannonball
Runs Parts destructive test.
Just bangs them on his iron skull
Picks out ones that test best.

Put Dog Boy as Security
He has the loudest bark.
To 'luminate obscurity
Brought in the Human Quark.

The Mars employees all look shocked:
Is this some kind of joke?
Has some folk up there gotten clocked
From some numb blockhead's poke?

They want us wearing sequined suits
To add a bit of snazz.
Would make us look like bowls of fruit
Can almost hear the razz.

They just installed a trampoline
To bounce from place to place.
Old Gerferd trampled-up his spleen
With his keen lack of grace.

It's hard to put on wheel lug nuts
With all this bouncing 'round.
The bumping by these bouncing butts
And squeezing out rude sound.

The Ringmaster did his own ads
Dressed in top hat, red coat.
"The new Mars Cars have new Mars fads
That might cause price to bloat."

Equipped cars with a dozen horns
Could honk out crazy tunes.
Like some dumb song 'bout cracking corns
Or "Yes, we have no prunes."

The cust'mers like the Whoopie seats
For 'bout 11 days.
By then, they look for air defeats
To turn-off this cute craze.

The cupholder, when loaded up
Plays "Pop Goes Weasel" tune.
When tune is done… best grab your cup
Cuz something's gettin' strewn.

An automatic popcorn pot
Is featured in the glove box.
It's better than what imports' got
In their econo-love-box.

Forced rear glass wipers must be bought
On every station wagon.
Said "It's for Safety"… but all thought
Liked look of tail waggin'.

They came out with the "Nutshell" coupe
One color scheme:  Beach Ball
Too small to load a hula hoop
When floored, would often stall.

Would sell to the fuel-conscious crowd
Who wanted "fun", not speed.
For folks, when asked what makes them proud,
"Size" was not avowed need.

But this "fun" car was not so fun
Was un-fun drive, at best.
'Bout needed one swift push to run
Up hills to cross a crest.

So Nutshells filled up Dealer lots
And rotted in the sun.
Mars Distribution formed large clots
As bystanders poked fun.

Mars engines redesigned to burn
Rich mix of el'phant waste.
Recycle nasty beasty churn
To make a fast-burn paste.

Spent years/careers perfecting how
To sell cow dung to masses.
Would now use this for engine chow
With its rich octane gases.

Was tough to atomize the poop
And break up little chunks.
Mixed in with hairballs from the scoop...
So, who let out the skunks?

The bio-fuel worked good at first
Despite bad exhaust fume.
But later, their gas bubble burst
Loomed trouble with "the Broom".

The Broom, a screen in exhaust flow
There to scrub burnt poo-clumps.
But tended to plug-up, and so
Would give the Mars the mumps.

Caused engines to then overheat
The Mars Cars would get parked.
While owners cursed, took to their feet
And fireworks were sparked.

The Leaders said: <u>Enough</u> of this.
These engined cars aren't fun.
Next thing they'll want to run on piss
These potty cars can't run.

Converted Mars to make <u>Play Cars</u>.
Now targeted at kids.
That look like pedaled mason jars
With easy-opening lids.

The Mars Czar quit and headed home
To circuses he knew.
To Marks beneath the big-top dome
Who he <u>knew</u> how to screw.

Back to his 3-ring comfort zone
To tents of far less frown.
Where his persuasive groans had grown
To one big sucking sound.

# Bribers Bay

She'd tossed and turned all through the night
To get one lousy wink.
While hampered by Joe Snoreville's Right
Of Passage mass o'stink.

Was that a dream?  It seemed so real…
Could almost feel the touch.
Recall some guy with suit of teal
Now <u>that</u> was Fashion Grudge.

What was that store name…Bribers Bay?
Trays full of bribes for sale?
That loud mouth upfront… what'd he say
From perch beyond the pail?

> Step right into our "Bribe Town" store
> And pick an aisle that works.
> But please don't call our Storekeep "whore"
> Cuz he deplores your smirks.

> Our "Quick Bribe" counter lets you see
> The new hot bribes on sale.
> Where Briber can link with Bribee
> On any size or scale.

She drifts off to redream the dream
Half-sleeping, half-awake.
Half seeing this intriguing scheme
Of wise guys on the take.

Drifts near Bribe counter to eavesdrop
Hears deal that's close to closing.
Someone will get some cream of crop,
Some other will get hosing:

> Step up… We have a <u>Budget Vote</u>
> On sale for just one Cruise
> Plus one size-4 chinchilla coat…
> A deal you just can't lose!
>
> Or this peach… one long House floor speech
> 'Bout getting guns controlled.
> Five skins to keep guns out of reach…
> Six, if you want more sold.

"It's fascinating," she observes
"To see this frenzied pace.
Of bribe-aholics full of verve
Who seem to lack disk space."

Looks down the hall, next to men's stall
A small-size Lobby Lobby
Tight packed, hired-guns squished wall to wall
Who aggravate, as hobby.

Who flow with how the wind might blow
Or just blow wind themselves.
Unsure what they pretend to know
But know they don't want delves.

They used to be on other side
Slicked-up in prestige office.
So now they know the Pricing side
Claim: "Inside guys won't scoff us."

She scans the room, engulfed in fog
Bribe dealing in thick mist.
With players who just love the bog
Not worried if they're hissed.

    In back, she sees Bribe Match Dot Com…
    With PC's on the right.
    Perusing options, choosing from
    Some full Bribes or Bribes Light.

    There's Jenkins… he just made a match…
    New tax incentive bill.
    He needed poison pills attached
    To hatch a tax dodge drill.

    Jenks ponied-up Aruba trips
    For Shmipps and his 3 kids.
    They claimed it was to "inspect ships
    That have gone out for bids."    (ha ha)

O'er there… a Mark-down, past 3 weeks
For regs on Acid Rain.
A challenge:  moving regs for freaks
Who go 'round sniffing drains.

But sniffers have a lot of stash
They'd squirreled back from the 60's.
Back when they weren't too stoned or crashed
On field trips chasing pixies.

Downstairs, meets guy with paltry funds
Who's flustered, verge of fail.
She says:  Serve up 10 bakery buns,
They might read your email.

Make it one nice fresh apple pie
They'll read Attached proposal.
But if the pie crust's burnt or dry
Both end up in Disposal.

   Did I say what I think I said?
   Some graft of apple pie?
   Advising how a bribe is bred
   Into one astute buy?         (oh my!)

She spots her old friend George McFlunn.
One billionaire who's bored.
Will buy influence by the ton
Today… appears he's scored.

To him, it's like a Vegas game
She knows ole George loves craps
Would "Don't" play, so when his Come came
He'd feign a lame collapse.

But now he's on the inside track
Can now bet <u>with</u> the dice.
He's pushing in his whole chip stack…
This ain't no game for mice.

George just bought something really big
But is not letting on
She knows he did a wallet dig
Big gig he's betting on.

Walks upstairs where Bribe Auction starts
Fine earmarks up for bid.
They line up with their goodies carts
And open up the lid.

They're bidding on a highway bill
I- nine hundred —o- six
That goes from Bilgeville's Garbage Hill
To Melvin's House of Bricks.

All want it in their own backyard
Build motels on the cheaps.
With Cracker Barrels, Quickie Mart
And dump that sells used Jeeps.

New jobs, new roads, new freebie dough
Would pour into their town.
The bidding's started pretty low
See what their chums choke down.

    The hawker shouts: "He's the <u>swing vote</u>!"
    You need to empty pockets
    Serve up more than some family goat
    Or useless box of sprockets.

Can't "guarantee" he'll vote your way
Cuz (wink, wink) that's illegal.
But there's good chance... will go your way
If you show us more Eagle.

Then... guy serves up a new Corvette.
Next: tuxxed butler for life
New bid... a brand new Gulfstream jet
Then: Shrink to cure your strife.

Announced... we have a Winner, friends.
The Strife-beater has won!
No clock on how much time he spends
To manufacture fun.

Next up for bid: Term Limit bill...
By some incumbent coot.
But this old bird will need to fill
His gill before the boot.

So Grampaw needs a pretty price...
High time to up-the-pony
To unclench this unflinching vise
Gripped by this class of crony.

She walks before the bidding starts
Has just 'bout had enough.
A gut well-filled with bribing tarts
Topped with marshmallow fluff.

And as she walks back toward the door
Sees bribers wiped, bribed-out.
She wonders: did these bribers score?
Or did their bribes crap out?

Alarm clock breaks her from the trance
Sweat rumbles off her head
She gives old Onion Joe a glance
Then stumbles out of bed.

Still thinking 'bout her strange transport
That's ached her frontal lobe.
But soon heads downtown to her court
Where there, she'll don her robe.

# Labelmania

Deflabenheimer donned her coat
And hurried in her lab.
So anxious to observe the float
Of this new dab she'd fabbed.

Could this be breakthrough she had dreamed
For 'bout a thousand days?
The testing and investing schemed
To snake through this tough maze?

Eureka!  Chloro-keedron split
Extracted from Lean feed
And porogated omni-twit
From that deplungant seed!!

Deflab just found the magic key
A challenge centuries old
Discovered by sheer mastery
A cure for <u>Common Cold.</u>

Had taken years of diligence
Some rants and screams aloud
More hard work than intelligence
Tom Edison'd be proud.

But now...Voila!!  Concocted pill
A task so darn laborious
A need that she can now fulfill
Deflab's emerged victorious.

It took a myriad of weeks
To do tests, get approval
And guard against sneak info leaks
In market tests in Shmooville.

And when the testing was complete
One side-effect, one hitch
If gulp a pill in too much heat
Could cause arm pits to itch.

Found this outcome in 2 percent
Blew off as:  Peanut Stand.
But sent it up to get consent
From bland old Legal Land

The lawyers skilled in panic time
And covering butts beaucoup
Then shifted into Manic time
With quakes up their gazoo.

You <u>must</u> attach a warning tag
To warn of Arm Pit Itch
A glitch like this must twitch a flag
To wag in every pitch.

For Arm pit itch??  You surely jest!!
For one ingested pill?
You Lawyers' zest is overdressed
Your quest is sounding shrill.

But lawyers went on further still
Explored the chance of scratch:
What if there's scratching willy-nill?
What if some scratch should snatch?

Then open skin for germ infect
And if that scrape's severe?
They'll need to get their scratchings checked
Keep penicillin near.

And if infection's too advanced
Will need go to E.R.
And there to be disrobed, de-pantsed
Get served at I.V. bar

Put all this on the Warning Tag
And note the chance of staph
And just might cause the eyes to bag
A groin pull if you laugh.

Apply some Calamine…?  Might have
An allergy reaction.
A rash outbreak from all this salve
Might cause mass skin compaction.

Another Legal mind weighed-in
What if the sweat glands swelled?
If hyperthermia swayed in
Cuz perspiration quelled?

The patient could go into shock
Get dizzy, slump, or faint
Dehydrate like a desert rock
Turn 13 shades of paint.

These cold cure users must be warned
Before onset of chills
Warn now, so users won't be mourned
Cuz they popped Quick Cure pills.

Pill bottles had to be enlarged
To billboard mega-labels
Two sizes:  Large and Giga-large
The latter moved by cables.

They added:  Liver damage "Tssssk"
With no real evidence
But figured:  Hey, why take risk.
Let's stay on the Defense.

These warnings cover our bare cans
Let's cover our cans good.
Make sure each person understands
Slim chances understood.

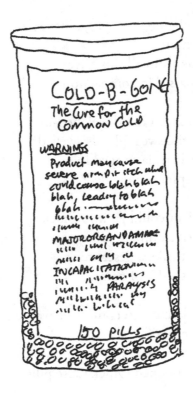

The TV ads for Cold-B-Gone
Had 10 secs of Brand glitz
And 50 secs of warning yawn
That stemmed from itchy pits.

Ads droned and droned with verbage crawl
But gave no sense of scope
The probability so small
You'd need a microscope.

But Focus Groups said it's a scare
To say the least, weren't sold.
"Don't want some transplant of my hair.
I'd rather have a cold."

Would not buy:  It's just Arm pit itch.
Would not trust:  Will Not Harm.
Think:  Snake oil from some charmless witch.
Set off the Smoke alarm.

Was technically a major cure
Up there with Jonas Salk.
Test markets made its prospects poor
Because of Lawyer balk.

The Lawyers breathed sighs of relief
Had foreseen griefs of suits
Seems like their briefs were just too brief
To see through all their moots.

The Drug firm CEO was cranked
Struck with one flabby tab.
Told Counsel:  You clowns must be thanked
For this yanked power grab.

Why bother with Analysis
Statistics, "complex" math?
Let's invoke plain paralysis
Give Cold Cure one cold bath!

Then throw the baby down the drain
With bath wash and debris
Because poor Egbert's got a stain
From bathing in your pee.

But lawyers said: You're welcome, Sir...
Appreciate your thump...
Cuz, frankly, we just save your fur
That covers your vast rump.

Hey, we can gear for mass tort suits
More money in our pockets.
Can flash-dance with pit-itching brutes
In endless court room dockets.

We'll move your La-Z-Boy to court
Cuz they'll go after you.
Not see that you're a nice old sport
Who simply "never knew".

Might could have meant a Nobel Prize
Instead it found the ditch.
Became food for the swarms of flies
Who might get wing-pit itch.

They shut the pilot process down
And burned up Deflab's notes.
They transferred Deflab out of town
To Land of Heavy Coats.

They pulled each bottle off the shelf.
They'd rebate bottles sold.
But Deflab kept some for herself
And never caught a cold.

And folks start noticing their pits
Start'd itching anyway.
Some airborne spore might've caused these fits
But then it went away.

# Sponge-ivity

The scientists just scratched their heads
How could they miss this trend?
Could be were on too many meds?
No time now to pretend.

But clearly now they see the light
Their glasses now defogged.
A late blast of profound insight
Got stubborn drains unclogged.

The population of the Sponge
Had grown beyond the threshold.
There's talk now that we must expunge
These varmints with this death-hold.

They've plunked themselves in river beds
And cluster in the millions
Then open pores in porous heads
Suck water by the billions.

Up to the point where raging brooks
Get shrunk to piddly streams.
Quaint little ponds in dreamy nooks
Turn into desert scenes.

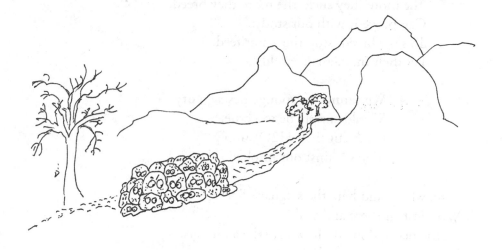

So now there's less for all the rest
Put rest on verge of drought.
A situation most detest
'Cept Sponge-lovers, no doubt.

But Sponge-lovers live up the hill
Their water's not at risk
Don't care much how much stream they spill
Won't stop from streaming brisk.

Sponge-ologists from 'cross the land
Convene for heavy noodle.
Broke 'way from their large box of sand
And notepads full of doodle.

Have undisputed facts, they show
About Sponge reproduction
That correlates with water flow
Inside their sponge-bank suction.

The more they suck, the more they breed.
Can prove it with our study.
To slow breed, stop the water feed.
Let their intakes get muddy.

We cannot let sponge nests go dry
Would simply be too cruel.
Can't cut their H2O supply
That's 'gainst our implied rule.

Sure, who could hate the stagnant Sponge
Who just sit there and soak?
Don't splash, don't dash, won't take a plunge
If over-doused, don't choke.

If not for Sponge, we'd never thought
Of how to wash our cars.
How would we clean the random splott
The mottled glopps and tars?

Those fuzzy little bulky mounds
Too cute to risk this kill.
The Sponge won't take this lying down…
On second thought…they will.

Let's give to them a Hobson's choice
Suck less, much less, or None.
May not expect Sponge to rejoice
When staring down that gun.

The Pro-Sponge and the Pro-Life talks
Went on for 2 more days.
Each compromise was met with balks
And gestured hand displays.

Pro-Spongers brought out scissors, saws…
"What if we cut yours off?"
Pro-Lifers brought out prunes and straws
Made sucking sounds and coughs.

And images…Sponge run amok
Who've squeegied every creek.
A cataclysmic water suck
Which caused Pro-Sponge to freak.

They put away their blades and said:
"Okay, we'll reconsider.
Let Sponges be a wee less-fed.
Squelch need for baby-sitter."

Found ways to divert river flow
So Sponge became less-sponge.
Friends taught the Sponges how to blow
Learn tricks how to expunge.

Try as they might, with programs/plans
It did not do much good
Cuz Sponges are just sponges, Fans
Won't un-sponge if they could.

Then soon denoted shifting trend
Sponge births were on decline.
A pop drop at each river bend
Old Grampaw Sponge was dyin'.

The decreased water dried their eggs
And parched their sponge-icles.
It made them wish that they had legs
To fend off grunge-icles

As Sponge appendages go dry
Main Sponge parts start to shrivel
Their spry turned into let-me-lie
Copped attitudes uncivil.

Meanwhile, Sponge-ologists assessed
Effects of this trimmed flow.
Ran every procreation test
That all Sponge experts know.

"Significant birth trend-line dip,"
Their interim report.
"Activity – a profound slip
Their whips are getting short."

Confirmed what everybody knew
Restated obvious.
Concluded really nothing new
Seemed like some lobbyist.

More outrage from the gang up-hill
While wading in their pools.
The whining, at times, got quite shrill
Still triple-flushing stools.

But, at some point, the Leaders said:
Why don't you  @#!&*%  shut up?
If wanna help, get off your lead
Downsize your coffee cup.

Those coffee cups did not downsize
Nor was there drain of pool.
But silenced all the wise chastise
Replies of the uncool.

Time passed.  Sponge learned how to adapt
And sponged a little less.
Their growth curve being sharply capped
Entrapped under duress.

And downstream, life had now revived.
The ponds would now refill.
They did not care this was contrived
Just lined up quick to swill.

SMOD

# Gleeps v. Gronks, part two

The Smods had stirred the Gronk and Gleep
With threats of pulling plugs
Of dousing governmental creep
And squelching favorite thugs.

Antithesis of both their views
This theory:  Sit on hands
This dreary:  Put the car on Cruise
To sit for all we stand.

    The Gronk and Gleep teams both agreed
    Hey…politics is fun.
    To dig and find things disagreed
    Not sure who's ever won.

    But these Smods are from different breeds
    Clods miss the point of game.
    It's not about which side succeeds
    Or which lame brain to blame.

No, it's about bein' in the ring
To fight and mix it up.
To spout that sting...that supreme zing...
Then watch them fix it up.

Both sides had recognized the risk
That apathy could bring.
Their counter-move would need be brisk
B'fore Smod-talk starts to cling.

So both sides gulped hard...then joined hands
In search of Common Ground.
Amazingly, they learned to dance
Surprising finds they found.

Agreed:  Advance in sensible ways
New laws must all make sense
Cannot go on a spending craze
Will watch each pound and pence.

Will care for folk that truly need
A helping hand when down
Will watchdog any outright greed...
Include greed in <u>this</u> town.

Support the king, on both our sides
And help the king succeed.
Tone down the grumbles, gripes, and chides
No more piranha feed.

Support, build-up our industry
Producing high-pay jobs
Don't cause key businesses to flee
For fear of resource robs.

Resist all tempts to go to war
Unless we get attacked.
Let's know what we are fighting for
And base it on true fact.

Squelch out the threat of Nothingness
That apathetic bunch
Of Smod-agendas we can't guess
Who're taking 'way our lunch.

So Gleeps and Gronks, with arm-in-arm
Veered on this all new tack.
Both confident: would do no harm...
Might get us in the Black.

And Smods moped for 'bout 15 secs
Then just gave one big shrug
Proceeded back to lounge on decks
Once they refilled their mugs.

ROBERT THOMAS is an engineer, and executive in the U.S. manufacturing industry who has worked in a variety of small and large companies. He is a keen observer of business practices, current events, people behaviors, triumphs, and struggles, and finds inklings of humor in the daily grind of it all. He has an off-beat, sometimes bizarre sense of humor, loves sarcasm and satire. The author enjoys storytelling, has been an amateur humorist for many years, but this is his first published work. He lives in Savannah, Georgia, and loves the richness of life in this beautiful southern town. He runs a blog and website at www.bizarreville. com which features more zany satire in an obtuse corner of the world. Please stop by for a visit and check out the shenanigans that could only happen in a place called bizarreville.

Printed in the United States
by Baker & Taylor Publisher Services